T0247141

TRENDS IN SOUTHEAST ASIA

PROSPERITY OR PREDICAMENT?

Decoding Certification Challenges in Malaysia's Palm Oil Industry

Serina Rahman and Lee Poh Onn

ISSUE

6

2024

YUSOF ISHAK
INSTITUTE

Published by: ISEAS Publishing
                  30 Heng Mui Keng Terrace
                  Singapore 119614
                  publish@iseas.edu.sg
                  http://bookshop.iseas.edu.sg

© 2024 ISEAS – Yusof Ishak Institute, Singapore

ISEAS Library Cataloguing-in-Publication Data

Name(s): Serina Rahman, author. | Lee, Poh Onn, author.
Title: Prosperity or predicament? Decoding certification challenges in Malaysia's palm oil industry / by Serina Rahman and Lee Poh Onn.
Description: Singapore : ISEAS – Yusof Ishak Institute, March 2024. | Series: Trends in Southeast Asia, ISSN 0219-3213 ; TRS6/24 | Includes bibliographical references.
Identifiers: ISBN 9789815203349 (soft cover) | ISBN 9789815203356 (ebook PDF)
Subjects: LCSH: Oil palm—Malaysia. | Palm oil industry—Certification—Malaysia.
Classification: LCC DS501 I59T no. 6(2024)

Typeset by Superskill Graphics Pte Ltd
Printed in Singapore by Markono Print Media Pte Ltd

FOREWORD

The economic, political, strategic and cultural dynamism in Southeast Asia has gained added relevance in recent years with the spectacular rise of giant economies in East and South Asia. This has drawn greater attention to the region and to the enhanced role it now plays in international relations and global economics.

The sustained effort made by Southeast Asian nations since 1967 towards a peaceful and gradual integration of their economies has had indubitable success, and perhaps as a consequence of this, most of these countries are undergoing deep political and social changes domestically and are constructing innovative solutions to meet new international challenges. Big Power tensions continue to be played out in the neighbourhood despite the tradition of neutrality exercised by the Association of Southeast Asian Nations (ASEAN).

The **Trends in Southeast Asia** series acts as a platform for serious analyses by selected authors who are experts in their fields. It is aimed at encouraging policymakers and scholars to contemplate the diversity and dynamism of this exciting region.

THE EDITORS

Series Chairman:
 Choi Shing Kwok

Series Editor:
 Ooi Kee Beng

Editorial Committee:
 Daljit Singh
 Francis E. Hutchinson
 Norshahril Saat

Prosperity or Predicament? Decoding Certification Challenges in Malaysia's Palm Oil Industry

By Serina Rahman and Lee Poh Onn

EXECUTIVE SUMMARY

- Oil palm was brought to Malaysia from West Africa as part of British colonial agricultural development initiatives, but the refining of crude palm oil only began in the 1970s as part of the move by the Malaysian government to industrialize the country's agrarian economy.
- Malaysia is the world's second-largest producer of palm oil, after Indonesia. Both countries account for about 85 per cent of total exports. Incidentally, smallholders produce about 40 per cent of the total output of palm oil in Malaysia.
- The palm oil industry is mired in controversy. Global campaigns originating in Europe and the US have branded the crop the biggest cause of deforestation, with proposed bans to follow in December 2024.
- Certification has been proposed as the solution to address gaps in sustainability. Sabah is used as an illustrative case study of an effective approach for statewide certification using both the Malaysian Sustainable Palm Oil (MSPO) and Roundtable for Sustainable Palm Oil (RSPO) schemes.

Prosperity or Predicament? Decoding Certification Challenges in Malaysia's Palm Oil Industry

By Serina Rahman and Lee Poh Onn[1]

INTRODUCTION

Malaysia is the second largest producer of palm oil after Indonesia.[2] Together, these two countries account for about 85 per cent of total exports around the world. In 2022, Indonesia alone produced 51.33

[1] Serina Rahman is Associate Fellow at the ISEAS – Yusof Ishak Institute, Singapore and Lecturer at the Department of Southeast Asian Studies, National University of Singapore (NUS). Lee Poh Onn is Senior Fellow at the ISEAS – Yusof Ishak Institute. Both are in the Malaysia Studies Programme at the ISEAS – Yusof Ishak Institute. We are very grateful to various individuals from the Sabah Forest Department (Datuk Sam Mannan, Datuk Mashor Mohd Jaini, Mr Frederick Kugan), Forever Sabah (Ms Cynthia Low, Ms Mega M. Kumar, Ms Elisna Latik, Mr Rizlan Morsit, Mr Neville Yap), Wilmar International (Ms Perpetua George), Sime Darby Plantation Berhad (Mr Rashyid Redza), MPOCC (Mr Chew Jit Seng), RSPO (Ms Javin Tan), Independent Consultant (Ms Rosalie Corpuz) for speaking to us during our fieldwork in Sabah, Peninsular Malaysia, and Singapore. We are also grateful for feedback from Francis E. Hutchinson (ISEAS – Yusof Ishak Institute), Helena Varkkey (Universiti Malaya), and Leow Huey Chuen (UOB Kay Hian Malaysia) on an earlier version of this paper. We also thank Ooi Kee Beng for editing this submission. Any errors remaining are ours.

[2] For a political economy discussion on the oil palm industry in Indonesia, see Helena Varkkey, "Patronage Politics as a Driver of Economic Regionalisation: The Indonesian Oil Palm Sector and Transboundary Haze", *Asia Pacific Viewpoint* 53, no. 3 (2012): 314–29; Helena Varkkey, "Regional Cooperation, Patronage and the ASEAN Agreement on Transboundary Haze Pollution", *International Environmental Agreements: Politics, Law and Economics* 14, Issue 1 (2014): 65–81; and Helena Varkkey, *The Haze Problem in Southeast Asia: Palm Oil and Patronage* (London: Routledge, 2016).

million tonnes of output, while Malaysia produced 18.45 million tonnes.[3] A shortage of sunflower oil supplies arising from the Russia-Ukraine war, and Indonesia's export restrictions of palm oil due to domestic shortages in cooking oil, lowered worldwide supplies and led to a rise in palm oil prices. A prolonged labour shortage caused by COVID-19 restrictions on the entry of foreign labour also lowered oil palm production in Malaysia. These factors added pressure on prices and increased Malaysia's oil palm revenues (export of palm oil and palm-based products) from RM108,515 million in 2021 to RM137,891 million in 2022, an increase of about 27 per cent.[4]

This paper first discusses the economic significance of the Malaysian oil palm industry within the context of the agriculture sector, as well its significance to individual states. The history of oil palm is then discussed. The focus then moves to smallholders who are dependent on oil palm for their livelihoods. The political economy of palm oil is then examined in light of new European Union regulations requiring deforestation-free sources along manufacturing supply chains.[5] Sustainability certification is seen as a solution to these new obstacles to Malaysian exports, but there are myriad challenges involved. The Malaysian Sustainable Palm Oil (MSPO) certification system has been gaining ground, but has yet to attain full international recognition and acceptance. An alternative international standard by the Roundtable for Sustainable Palm Oil (RSPO) also has its issues, and this will also be examined in the paper. This will be followed by a case study on certification efforts in Sabah.

---

[3] Reuters, "Palm Oil Production in Top Asian Producers to Remain Tight in 2023", 13 January 2023, https://www.reuters.com/article/malaysia-palmoil-idUSKBN2TR0VP/ (accessed 20 October 2023).

[4] Ministry of Plantation and Commodities, "Data Statistics on Commodities 2022: Palm Oil, Malaysia: 2023", p. 24, https://www.kpk.gov.my/kpk/images/mpi_statistik/2023_statistik_on_commodity/Sawit_2023.pdf (accessed 15 November 2023).

[5] This was ratified in June 2023, but the laws will only be enforced in December 2024. Refer to https://environment.ec.europa.eu/news/green-deal-new-law-fight-global-deforestation-and-forest-degradation-driven-eu-production-and-2023-06-29_en

In 2022, agriculture contributed 6.6 per cent of total Malaysian GDP (Constant 2015 Prices), of which 2.4 per cent was from oil palm.[6] Agriculture is among Malaysia's top three sectors, with services (57 per cent) and manufacturing (24 per cent) contributing the most to annual GDP.[7] Oil palm alone contributed, on average, over 35 per cent of the total gross value of the agriculture sector from 2018 to 2022.[8]

Agriculture matters more to some states than others. In terms of the contribution of agriculture to total GDP, the top five states with the largest agriculture sectors are Johor (17.5 per cent), Sarawak (14.7 per cent), Pahang (13.8 per cent), Sabah (12.6 per cent) and Perak (11.4 per cent). This is shown in Figure 1. In Sabah and Sarawak, 32.8 per cent and 19.1 per cent of the labour force are employed in the agriculture sector of these states, respectively (as of end-2022).

History of Oil Palm

Oil palm was brought to Malaysia from West Africa as part of British colonial agricultural development initiatives, but the refining of crude palm oil only began in the 1970s as part of the move to industrialize Malaysia's agrarian economy. In the 1970s and 1980s, oil palm cultivation took place mainly in Peninsular Malaysia. However, as sizeable swathes of land slowly became unavailable for plantation agriculture on the peninsula, East Malaysia (beginning with Sabah and later Sarawak) became the centre of oil palm cultivation in the 1990s.[9]

---

[6] Department of Statistics Malaysia (DOSM), "Selected Agricultural Indicators 2023", October 2023, p. 36, https://www.dosm.gov.my/uploads/release-content/file_20231027103409.pdf (accessed 15 November 2023).

[7] Economic Planning Unit (EPU), Prime Minister's Department, "The Malaysian Economy in Figures 2022", revised as at June 2022, p. 1, https://www.ekonomi.gov.my/sites/default/files/2022-08/MEIF2022.pdf (accessed 15 November 2023).

[8] DOSM, "Selected Agricultural Indicators 2023", p. 39.

[9] Yumi Kato and Ryoji Soda, "The Impact of RSPO Certification on Oil Palm Smallholdings in Sarawak", in *Anthropogenic Tropical Forests: Advances in Asian Human-Environmental Research*, edited by N. Ishikawa and R. Soda (Singapore: Springer, 2020), p. 338; and Malaysian Oil Palm Statistics 2022, 42nd ed. (Selangor, Malaysia: Malaysian Palm Oil Board (MPOB), 2023), p. 3.

4

Figure 1: Contribution of Agriculture to Total GDP, Top Five States

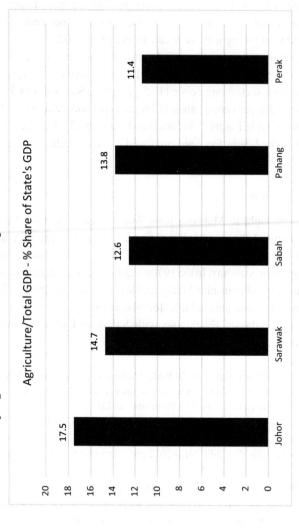

Source: Department of Statistics Malaysia (DOSM), "Selected Agricultural Indicators 2023", October 2023, p. 39, https://www.dosm.gov.my/uploads/release-content/file_20231027103409.pdf (accessed 15 November 2023).

In 1975, about 89 per cent of the total cultivated oil palm areas were in Peninsular Malaysia. This figure fell to 74 per cent in 1995, then 61 per cent in 2000. Incidentally, it was in 2006 that Indonesia overtook Malaysia as the largest palm oil producer. By 2010, the proportion of total cultivated palm oil areas in Peninsular Malaysia had decreased to only 55 per cent. In Sabah, however, the corresponding figure had grown to 31 per cent, and 14 per cent in Sarawak.[10] By 2020, the total cultivated area in the peninsula had decreased further to 47 per cent. There was also a decrease in Sabah, to 26 per cent, but an increase in Sarawak to 27 per cent (see Figure 2).

Two widely used certification standards exist in Malaysia: the nationally set Malaysian Sustainable Palm Oil (MSPO) Certification and the internationally set Roundtable for Sustainable Palm Oil (RSPO) Certification. Both standards will be examined in detail later in this paper.

SMALLHOLDERS IN THE OIL PALM INDUSTRY

In the last five years, the key palm oil-producing states have been Sabah, Sarawak, Pahang, Johor, and Perak (see Table 1 and Figure 3). Johor, Sarawak, and Sabah have the highest number of independent smallholders in the country, with each state facing its own unique set of issues and difficulties.[11] Sabah is the third largest exporter of palm oil after Indonesia and Peninsular Malaysia.[12]

---

[10] Calculated from *Malaysian Oil Palm Statistics 2022*, 42nd ed., p. 3.

[11] The discussion on Johor, Sarawak and Sabah draws from an earlier work by Serina Rahman, "Malaysian Independent Oil Palm Smallholders and Their Struggle to Survive 2020", *ISEAS Perspective*, no. 2020/144, 17 December 2020, pp. 5–7, https://www.iseas.edu.sg/wp-content/uploads/2020/12/ISEAS_Perspective_2020_144.pdf (accessed 15 November 2023).

[12] Frederick Kugan, "The Implementation of the Sabah Jurisdictional Certified Sustainable Palm Oil (JCSPO) Initiative: The Successes and Challenges", Webinar presented at ISEAS –Yusof Ishak Institute, 12 August 2022.

6

Figure 2: Malaysia: Oil Palm Planted Area, 1975–2022 (hectares)

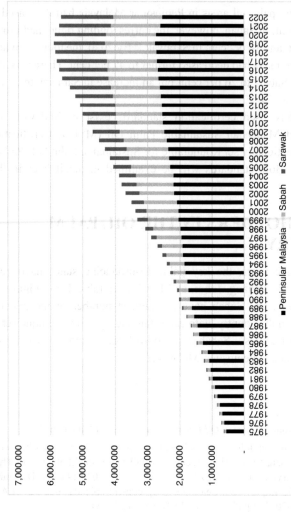

Source: Malaysian Oil Palm Statistics 2022, 42nd ed. (Selangor, Malaysia: Malaysian Palm Oil Board (MPOB), 2023), p. 3. See also Appendix 1.

Table 1: Distribution of Oil Palm Planted Area by State and Main Sectors, 2022

State	Estate and Organized Smallholders (ha)	Independent Smallholders (ha)	Total (ha)
Johor	529,511	147,342	676,853
Kedah	62,374	24,112	86,487
Kelantan	154,753	7,100	161,852
Melaka	42,564	9,783	52,347
Negri Sembilan	157,516	21,044	178,560
Pahang	709,270	40,543	749,813
Perak	272,299	79,799	352,098
Perlis	727	159	886
Pulau Pinang	3,285	5,294	8,579
Selangor	86,775	19,233	106,008
Terengganu	159,736	11,089	170,825
Peninsular Malaysia	*2,178,810*	*365,498*	*2,544,308*
Percentage (%)	85.6	14.4	100.0
Sabah	1,307,095	200,965	1,508,060
Percentage (%)	86.7	13.3	100.0
Sarawak	1,372,729	249,645	1,622,374
Percentage (%)	84.6	15.4	100.0
Total (Peninsular Malaysia and East Malaysia)	*4,858,634*	*816,107*	*5,674,742*
Percentage (%)	84.6	14.4	100.0

Source: Ministry of Plantation and Commodities, "Data Statistics on Commodities 2022: Palm Oil, Malaysia: 2023", p. 2, https://www.kpk.gov.my/kpk/images/mpi_statistik/2023_statistik_on_commodity/Sawit_2023.pdf (accessed 15 November 2023).

Figure 3: Production of Crude Palm Oil by State, 2018–22

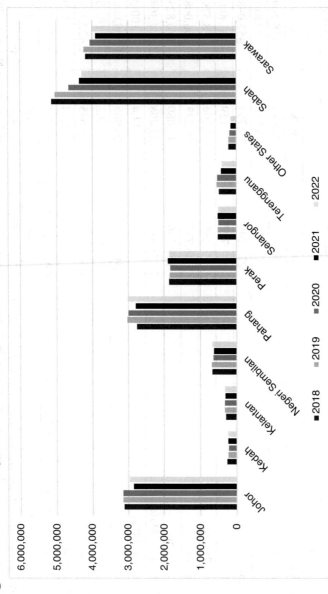

Note: In terms of production, 5.67 million hectares of oil palm produce about 18.45 million tonnes of crude palm oil and 4.55 million tonnes of palm kernel.

Source: Ministry of Plantation and Commodities, "Data Statistics on Commodities 2022: Palm Oil, Malaysia: 2023", p. 5, https://www.kpk.gov.my/kpk/images/mpi_statistik/2023_statistik_on_commodity/Sawit_2023.pdf (accessed 15 November 2023). See also Appendix 2.

Smallholders comprise farmers who own 100 acres of land or less (40.46 ha). In Malaysia, smallholder oil palm production makes up 40 per cent of all output (more than 300,000 individuals) and contributes about 18 million tonnes of palm oil production per year to the national total.[13] A significant portion of Malaysian oil palm is therefore produced by smallholders and anything that affects oil palm revenues would adversely affect their livelihoods. In terms of land area, smallholders in Malaysia occupy about 26.2 per cent of total oil palm areas, while plantations (private and government/state agencies) comprise 73.8 per cent of the 5.67 million ha (see Table 2 and Figure 4).

Table 2 breaks down hectarage into independent smallholders, organized smallholders, and private and government estates.

Table 2: Distribution of Oil Palm Planted Area by Category, 2022 and 2021

Category	2022 (ha)	2022 (%)	2021 (ha)	2021 (%)
Independent Smallholders	816,107	14.4	863,360	15.1
Organized Smallholders	667,868	11.8	672,986	11.7
Private and Government/State Agencies Estates	4,190,766	73.8	4,201,385	73.2
Total	5,674,741		5,737,731	100

Source: *Malaysian Oil Palm Statistics 2022*, 42nd ed. (Selangor, Malaysia: Malaysian Palm Oil Board (MPOB), 2023), p. 7.

---

[13] Malaysian Palm Oil Council, "The Oil Palm", https://theoilpalm.org/about/#Small_Farmers (accessed 30 November 2020).

Figure 4: Distribution of Oil Palm Planted Area by Category, 2022

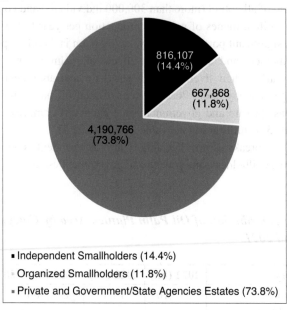

Source: *Malaysian Oil Palm Statistics 2022*, 42nd ed. (Selangor, Malaysia: Malaysian Palm Oil Board (MPOB), 2023), p. 7.

Oil palm smallholders are often estates owned by families (including their children) who depend on migrant labour in the harvesting process.[14] For them, oil palm is their primary source of cash income with consumption and subsistence crops grown alongside for food. Many smallholders are indigenous people (in both Peninsular and East Malaysia) who may or may not have formal land titles, although they may have been living and subsisting in these areas for many generations. These crops often suffer poor yields and use little or no technology. Environmental degradation

---

[14] The discussion here draws from Serina Rahman, "Malaysian Independent Oil Palm Smallholders and Their Struggle to Survive 2020", pp. 4–5.

by way of forest clearing, land burning and fertilizer is rampant. For farmers, oil palm is an attractive crop compared to other conventional crops. In fact, oil palm has an average yield of 3.72 tonnes/ha/year compared to 0.4 tonnes/ha/year for soybean, 0.55 tonnes/ha/year from sunflower, and 0.72 tonnes/ha/year for rapeseed.[15] Drawing from these yields, oil palm is nearly ten times more productive than soybean and five times more attractive than rapeseed.

In Malaysia, oil palm is seen as a means of poverty alleviation. Land resettlement schemes for oil palm cultivation under the Federal Land Development Authority (FELDA) have reduced the 50 per cent poverty rate that smallholder communities suffered in the 1960s to just 5 per cent today.[16] For many in rural areas, oil palm is the only way to meet needs which is not about harvesting from the wild; this has enabled many communities to put food on the table and their children through school.

Smallholders fall under two categories: organized or independent. Examples of organized smallholders include the FELDA schemes of Peninsular Malaysia and to a smaller extent, Sabah, as well as the Federal Land Consolidation and Rehabilitation Authority (FELCRA) (whole of Malaysia) or Rubber Industry Smallholders Development Authority (RISDA) (originally for rubber) schemes. The Sarawak Land Consolidation and Rehabilitation Authority (SALCRA) and Sabah Land Development Board (SLDB) are also government agencies that, like the others, support oil palm and rubber smallholders through resettlement and crop conversion schemes or other assistance. These schemes will be discussed in more detail in subsequent sections.

Organized smallholders are provided with technical assistance, agricultural inputs (seedlings, fertilizers, pesticides), and financing from relevant government agencies. However, they are then bound to send their crops to mills or intermediaries associated with these agencies and

---

[15] Kuok Ho Daniel Tang and Hamad M.S. Al Qahtani, "Sustainability of Oil Palm Plantations in Malaysia", *Environment Development and Sustainability* 22 (2020), p. 5016.

[16] Malaysian Palm Oil Council, "The Oil Palm".

are at times unable to obtain the best prices for their harvests. Independent smallholders usually cultivate crops with no external assistance. However, some may receive technical assistance via government extension services (such as Tunjuk Ajar dan Nasihat Sawit or TUNAS,[17] an assistance centre under the Malaysian Palm Oil Board (MPOB) for MSPO certification) or from large palm oil processing companies that purchase their oil palm fresh fruit bunches.

Many smallholders are therefore families who made the switch to oil palm from cash crops, which had otherwise served as a family's source of nutrition. This is especially so in remote rural and indigenous communities. RISDA also offers replanting subsidies for farmers who decide to switch to oil palm. FELDA and FELCRA began with social objectives to resettle and alleviate poverty through oil palm and have proven to be among the most successful government-led initiatives to organize and provide support to smallholders. There have also been several attempts at forming cooperatives to handle cash flows and access to markets, and myriad associations such as the National Association of Smallholders which work to provide a collective voice for small farmers.[18]

Despite the advantages offered by such initiatives, many oil palm smallholders remain independent. Some were initially under FELDA schemes but decided not to continue after the first fifteen-year maturity agreement, either in the hope of getting a better deal with independent

---

[17] TUNAS is an extension service offered by the MPOB to help independent smallholders, particularly for MSPO certification. In Malaysia, anyone who owns oil palm land less than 40.46 ha individually or collectively is considered to have an independent smallholding. In Sabah, the average size of a smallholding is 2.5 ha. See Yusman Bin Haruna, "MSPO Certification for Independent Smallholder in Sabah", MPOCC and MSPO, no date, https://www.mpocc.org.my/mspo-blogs/mspo-certification-for-independent-smallholder-in-sabah (accessed 15 November 2023).

[18] Serina Rahman, "Malaysian Independent Oil Palm Smallholders and Their Struggle to Survive 2020", p. 4.

millers or to avoid joint estate costs and fixed fertilizer charges. These smallholders opted out despite potentially lower yields.[19] In general, independent farmers have limited or no access to the wider market or millers, and are usually entirely dependent on middlemen who are willing to travel the distance to collect their ripe fresh fruit bunch harvests.[20] This also means that they have little or no support in terms of seeds, fertilizers and manpower.

Independent smallholders make up 0.82 million hectares (14.4 per cent) of total planted oil palm as of December 2022, while organized smallholders make up 11.8 per cent or 0.67 million hectares (see Table 1). In Sabah and Sarawak, the proportion of land areas under independent smallholders makes up 17.5 per cent of all cultivated areas.[21] Independent smallholders sell their crops directly to local mills or traders and are free to bargain to obtain the best price.[22] However, a study in Johor has shown that the yield per hectare of organized smallholders is less than that of independent smallholders (19 tonnes in contrast to 16–17 tonnes). In this instance, the net return per hectare was RM1,275 for organized smallholders as compared to RM1,212 for independent smallholders in 2005.[23]

[19] S. Vermeulen and N. Goad, *Towards Better Practice in Smallholder Palm Oil Production*, Natural Resource Issues Series No. 3 (London: International Institute for Environment and Development, 2006).

[20] The Mah Meri women of Pulau Carey were paid only RM3 (S$1) per sack of collected loose ripe fruit (those that fall off the fresh fruit bunches during harvest): personal communication, Reita Rahim, Gerai OA; Serina Rahman, "Malaysian Independent Oil Palm Smallholders and Their Struggle to Survive 2020", p. 4.

[21] *Malaysian Oil Palm Statistics 2022*, 42nd ed. (Selangor, Malaysia: Malaysian Palm Oil Board (MPOB), 2023), p. 8.

[22] Shaufique Fahmi Sidique, Tey Yeong Sheng, Marcel Djama, Che Ku Amir Rizal Che Ku Mohd, Diana Rose Sadili, and Syahaneem Mohamad Zainalabidin, *The Impacts of RSPO on the Livelihood of Smallholders: Case Studies in East Malaysia* (Kuala Lumpur: RSPO Secretariat Sdn Bhd, 2015), p. 2.

[23] Study cited in ibid., p. 2.

Johor

Johor has always been, and remains, an agricultural powerhouse, despite increasing urbanization and development across the state. Land has been cleared for rubber plantations and other crops since the 1800s, abetted by the state's extensive railway networks and access to international markets through Singapore. Hence, while deforestation is the oil palm industry's biggest bogeyman, this problem does not apply to Johor's smallholders, who simply switched to oil palm over time from other agricultural crops.[24] Tightened laws on illegal logging at both the state and federal levels have further neutralized this contention for the state.[25]

In 2015, more than half of Johor's land was used for agriculture, with almost 75 per cent dedicated to oil palm. This agricultural imprint is expected to expand until 2030 with oil palm planting expected to increase by another 13 per cent from its 2015 levels.[26] Johor has the highest number and acreage of independent smallholders in Peninsular Malaysia. A study of independent smallholders in Johor[27] showed that while there were lower costs and higher incomes compared to estate outputs, the yield was low, and many of the smallholdings were of mature crops with elderly owners. Farmers in Johor often struggle with low capital and manual labour—especially as their children often opt to work in nearby

---

[24] Geoffrey K. Pakiam, *Agriculture in Johor: What's Left?* Trends in Southeast Asia no. 19/2018 (Singapore: ISEAS – Yusof Ishak Institute, 2018), p. 21.

[25] This applies to inland forests but may not necessarily apply to riverine mangroves and peatlands which may still be cleared for oil palm as they do not fall under the "inland forest" category. Damage inflicted on mangrove forests and peatlands for oil palm and myriad other development projects however continue to occur in Johor.

[26] Pakiam, *Agriculture in Johor*, p. 34.

[27] A. Ismail, M.A. Simeh, and M. Mohd Noor, "The Production Cost of Oil Palm Fresh Fruit Bunches in the Case of Independent Smallholders in Johor", *Oil Palm Industry Economic Journal* 3, no. 1 (2003): 1–7, http://palmoilis.mpob.gov.my/publications/OPIEJ/opiejv3n1-1.pdf (accessed 30 November 2020).

big cities instead of on family farms. While some enterprising individuals help older landowners manage their farms,[28] many continue to struggle with new requirements for sustainability certification; only 4.2 per cent of Johor's independent smallholders are MSPO-certified.[29]

Sarawak

The legitimacy of land ownership is often the biggest problem for smallholders in East Malaysia. Indigenous communities, in particular, struggle with issues of land tenure, as indigenous ancestral lands are not necessarily recognized by state governments, even though the communities have lived, worked and died on them for generations.

Sarawak initiated "Konsep Baru" (New Concept) for rural land development in areas under native customary rights. This initiative resulted in indigenous communities retaining 30 per cent ownership over land, while 60 per cent goes to a selected plantation company to provide financial capital to develop land for palm oil. The remaining 10 per cent goes to the state government as power of attorney and trustee. The indigenous landowner loses all say in daily decision-making in the signing of the agreement, while the plantation company has a right to extend the agreement for another sixty years if there is no profit made. This scheme was highly contested by Sarawak's indigenous people, but land tenure uncertainty and controversy continue until today.[30] Disputes are nevertheless being resolved. Since 2010, over a million hectares of

---

[28] M. Taylor, "Too Late to Plant Green Seed Among World's Forgotten Palm Oil Farmers?", Thomson Reuters Foundation, 29 March 2018, https://www.reuters.com/article/us-asia-palmoil-environment-farming- idUSKBN1H504O.

[29] *Malay Mail*, "Minister—55pc of Nation's Oil Palm Plantation MSPO-Certified", 11 November 2019, https://www.malaymail.com/news/malaysia/2019/11/11/minister-55pc-of-nations-oil-palm-plantation-mspo- certified/1808990 (accessed 12 November 2019).

[30] Vermeulen and Goad, *Towards Better Practice in Smallholder Palm Oil Production*.

native customary rights (NCR) land have been surveyed. This compares to the period 1960 to 2010 where only 260,000 ha were surveyed.[31]

Several NGOs work with communities and local leaders to verify and negotiate land titles with state land and forestry departments as part of national efforts to attain sustainability certification. One of the main obstacles to attaining certification by either the MSPO or the RSPO for all smallholders, however, is the need to provide proof of land tenure.

In a study by Kato and Soda (2020) on Sarawak smallholdings, it was found that a single smallholding could each earn an income of between RM3,255 to RM3,320 per month based on the average price of RM600 per tonne of fresh fruit bunch.[32] These calculations were based on plantings of 2,000 palm trees by smallholdings of between 11.1 ha to 12.5 ha. On average, 170 palm trees were planted in each hectare of land. Villagers have said that they could make a decent living with just a total of 500 palm trees (about 3 ha of land) and would live quite comfortably with 1,000 palm trees. This amount means that they would not need to grow rice to supplement their income. Even if these villagers wanted to grow rice, they would not have enough time and labour to attend to rice planting, given the work required to tend to their oil palm plantation.[33] The most important factors for smallholding success are access to road networks, transport systems, multiple buyers and appropriate agricultural training.[34]

Many villagers in this Sarawak case study used to earn income by selling vegetables, corn and wild boar meat at nearby markets, besides planting wet and dry rice in the 1950s. In the second half of the 1950s, they started planting rubber trees and sold the harvested latex a few

---

[31] *Borneo Post Online*, "Over a Million Hectares of NCR Land in Sarawak Surveyed under New Initiative since 2010", 17 October 2021, https://www.theborneopost.com/2021/10/17/over-a-million-hectares-of-ncr-land-in-sarawak-surveyed-under-new-initiative-since-2010/ (accessed 1 January 2024).

[32] Kato and Soda, "The Impact of RSPO Certification on Oil Palm Smallholdings in Sarawak", pp. 348–49.

[33] Ibid., p. 349.

[34] Ibid., p. 349.

decades later. In the 1980s, they started cultivating cocoa and coffee, but neither of these crops provided stable sources of income. The planting of black pepper, however, helped to supplement their incomes. In the 1990s and early 2000s, logging provided an attractive and alternative source of income as many villagers also worked away from their farms in logging companies. In recent years villagers have started working in oil palm plantations in addition to planting oil palm in their own smallholdings.[35]

Sabah

Sabah produces 10 per cent of the world's palm oil but remains one of Malaysia's poorest states and with the highest levels of absolute poverty.[36] About 96 per cent of Sabah's oil palm plantations are MSPO-certified and 26 per cent RSPO-certified by 2022.[37] Many smallholder families live under the national poverty line, earning an average of RM1,600 (SG$533) per month.[38] notwithstanding the environmental controversies that surround oil palm, it is this crop that helps communities scrape through financial difficulties, providing between one-third to half of a household's income (Forever Sabah, 2018). A smallholder's median income in Sabah is RM1,500 (SG$500) per month; 92 per cent of those studied by Forever Sabah reported that this was not enough to cover their basic needs. The reality, however, is that the hurdles of certification may now actually leave them in deeper difficulty than before.

---

[35] Ibid., pp. 344–49.

[36] This is based on the revised poverty line figure of RM2,208. Refer to I. Lim, "Statistics Dept: Malaysia's New Poverty Line Income Is RM2,208, over 400k Households Considered Poor", *Malay Mail*, 10 July 2020, https://www.malaymail.com/news/malaysia/2020/07/10/statistics-dept-malaysias-new-poverty-line-income-is- rm2208-over-400k-house/1883285

[37] Kugan, "The Implementation of the Sabah Jurisdictional Certified Sustainable Palm Oil (JCSPO) Initiative".

[38] The average Malaysian independent smallholder (often a subsistence farmer) has only 3.9 ha of land. Refer to: R. Senawi, N.K. Rahman, N. Mansor, and A. Kuntum, "Transformation of Oil Palm Independent Smallholders through Malaysian Sustainable Palm Oil", *Journal of Oil Palm Research* (2019). https://doi.org/10.21894/jopr.2019.0038

In an initiative led by the state Forestry Department,[39] Sabah worked to apply the RSPO's jurisdictional approach for statewide oil palm certification. This approach allows smallholders to pool resources and share facilities as well as benefit from communal training and support to attain certification. Many smallholders do not understand the requirements for oil palm certification; some are not even aware of the existence of MSPO and RSPO. This difficulty is compounded by the inability of certifying bodies to translate those requirements into a language that rural and indigenous communities can comprehend.[40] While there may be a bounty of information online, a lack of telephone or Internet access and at times, illiteracy, makes it difficult for rural communities to get to and use available online resources. NGOs have reported that some indigenous communities were made to believe that without certification, they would not be able to sell their harvests at all.[41]

The Malaysian government's efforts to project a sustainable face to its oil palm industry may make conditions more difficult for smallholders, especially if the proclaimed certification assistance[42] does not reach

---

[39] In 2015 Datuk Sam Mannan, then Sabah Forestry Department director, announced Sabah's goal to be a Certified Sustainable Palm Oil (CSPO) state, with all oil palm industry members certified under the RSPO by 2021. This was the beginning of the implementation of the RSPO jurisdictional approach to certification in Sabah (personal communication: Datuk Sam Mannan, 2016 and fieldwork in July 2018 in Sabah). There are those who disagree with the effectiveness of this approach however (and its necessary superiority to MSPO certification). Refer to S. Amarthalingam, "RSPO Is One Man's Wish List", *The Edge Markets*, 14 November 2017, https://www.theedgemarkets.com/article/rspo-one-mans-wish-list; and J. Watts, D. Nepstad, and S. Irawan, "Can Jurisdictional Certification Curb Palm Oil Deforestation in Indonesia (Commentary)", *Mongabay.com*, 19 July 2019, https://news.mongabay.com/2019/07/can-jurisdictional-certification-curb-palm-oil-deforestation-in-indonesia/

[40] Personal communication: July 2018, fieldwork in Sabah—interviews with oil palm industry members and relevant agency staff.

[41] Personal communication: Reita Rahim, Gerai OA (July 2020).

[42] Refer to *The Edge Markets*, "Over RM100 mil Allocated to Assist Smallholders Get MSPO Certification", 4 August 2019, https://www.theedgemarkets.com/article/over-rm100-mil-allocated-assist-smallholders-get-mspo- certification

the most rural of farmers. This purported "sustainability" is hence not inclusive or authentically sustainable.

One new worrying concern for the Malaysian oil palm industry is the ageing of oil palm trees (see Table 3).[43] The MPOC has estimated that there are 664,000 ha or about 12 per cent of the total land area where trees are aged 25 years and above. By 2027, over one-third of planted oil palm in Malaysia will be considered old. The average cost of replacing palm trees is about RM20,000 (US$4,265) per ha, or almost US$3 billion to replace all trees over 25 years old. Again, it will not be the plantations that will suffer the most, but the smallholders.

THE POLITICAL ECONOMY OF OIL PALM IN MALAYSIA AND EXPORT CHALLENGES

The palm oil industry is mired in controversy. Global campaigns originating in Europe and the US have branded the crop the biggest cause of deforestation;[44] an accusation vividly illustrated by viral videos of a lone orangutan trying to fend off an oncoming bulldozer.[45] Aside from both floral and faunal biodiversity loss, other allegations in the long list of environmental violations by the oil palm industry include the draining of peat swamps for plantations; the use of open burning to clear land and expired crops which lead to transboundary haze; the seizure of

---

[43] *South China Morning Post*, "Malaysia and Indonesia's Oil Palms are Getting Old—and That's Becoming a Multibillion Problem", 3 October 2023, https://www.scmp.com/news/asia/southeast-asia/article/3236593/malaysia-and-indonesias-oil-palms-are-getting-old-and-thats-becoming-multibillion-dollar-problem# (accessed 15 November 2023).

[44] These have culminated in new laws that may require the declaration of oil palm in consumer products, which could harm Southeast Asian exports. Refer to A. Anuar, "The Pitfalls of Malaysia's Palm Oil Defence", *East Asia Forum*, 22 August 2019, https://www.eastasiaforum.org/2019/08/22/the-pitfalls-of-malaysias-palm-oil-defence/

[45] International Animal Rescue video posted on 5 June 2018 (World Environment Day): https://www.youtube.com/watch?v=hT5xSwdvi8E

Table 3: Area under Oil Palm (Matured and Immature) by State, 2022 (hectares)

State	Mature (ha)	Immature (ha)	Total (ha)
Johor	631,478	45,375	676,853
Kedah	75,281	11,206	86,487
Kelantan	139,367	22,485	161,852
Melaka	48,056	4,290	52,347
Negeri Sembilan	167,461	11,099	178,560
Pahang	678,373	71,440	749,813
Perak	324,473	27,624	352,098
Perlis	883	3	886
Pulau Pinang	8,441	138	8,579
Selangor	96,282	9,726	106,008
Terengganu	141,337	29,487	170,825
Peninsular Malaysia	2,311,432	232,875	2,544,307
Sabah	1,326,940	181,120	1,508,060
Sarawak	1,488,917	133,458	1,622,374
East Malaysia	2,815,857	314,578	3,130,435

Source: *Malaysian Oil Palm Statistics 2022*, 42nd ed. (Selangor, Malaysia: Malaysian Palm Oil Board (MPOB), 2023), p. 6.

indigenous land without free and prior informed consent (FPIC); and myriad human rights abuses in the use of illegal migrant and child labour.

In response, oil palm proponents have accused the global north of trade protectionism, implying that the allegations were meant to boost demand for their own vegetable oils made from soy, sunflower and rapeseed. Published research[46] contests that livestock farming clears

---

[46] Note that these publications are hosted by oil palm industry-friendly journals such as the *Journal of Oil Palm, Environment and Health, and the Journal of Oil Palm Research* (to name a few), and there is little acknowledgement of sources of funding or backgrounds/affiliations of the researchers.

more forests and has a larger impact on the environment, and that oil palm in fact sequesters carbon, offsetting its burden on global warming.[47] Some publications also posit that oil palm plantations in fact support biodiversity.[48] This is a claim that is often corroborated by those who work and live in and around oil palm plantations; they describe how orangutans and other wildlife enter these areas to eat the fruit before returning to surrounding forests to sleep.[49]

Among the issues related to the bad press facing Malaysian oil palm is the use of peatlands for oil palm plantations. Peatlands constitute approximately 7.45 per cent or 2,457,730 ha of the total land area in Malaysia. Out of this, 69 per cent are found in Sarawak, 26 per cent in Peninsular Malaysia, and 5 per cent in Sabah.[50] In the early 2000s, it was estimated that the expansion of oil palm plantations caused a loss of about 6 per cent of tropical peatlands (approximately 880,000 ha) in Peninsular Malaysia, Borneo and Sumatra. By 2009, 666,038 ha of peatlands had been converted to palm oil plantations (about 27 per cent of all peatlands) in Sarawak. Sarawak had the highest proportion of oil palms planted in peatland areas (37.5 per cent) followed by Peninsular Malaysia (8.29 per cent).[51]

In terms of major export commodities, oil palm provided a revenue of RM15 billion, second only to liquefied natural gas (LNG), which was RM35 billion in 2021.[52] While timber production may have driven initial

---

[47] Y. Basiron and F.K. Yew, "Land Use Impacts of the Livestock and Palm Oil Industries", *Journal of Oil Palm, Environment and Health* 6 (2015).

[48] E.B. Fizherbert, J. Matthew, M.J. Struebig, A. Morel, F. Danielson, C.A. Bruhl, P.F. Donald, and B. Phalan, "How Will Oil Palm Expansion Affect Biodiversity?", *Trends in Ecology and Evolution* 23, no. 10 (2008).

[49] Personal communication: fieldwork July 2018 in Sabah—interviews with oil palm NGOs and relevant state agencies.

[50] Tang and Al Qahtani, "Sustainability of Oil Palm Plantations in Malaysia", p. 5009.

[51] Ibid., p. 5009.

[52] *Sarawak Facts and Figures 2022* (Sarawak: Economic Planning Unit Sarawak, Department of the Premier of Sarawak, 2022), p. 30.

deforestation from 1974 in different parts of Malaysia till its peak in 1993, oil palm expansion could have been the major driver of deforestation in Malaysia from the 2000s.[53] Tang and Qahtani (2000) cite a study by Global Watch where 7.29 million ha of tree cover was lost between 2001 and 2017, largely due to commodity-driven deforestation (oil palm).[54] In the earlier years, however, deforestation was driven mainly by timber (till the late 1980s), and after that by both timber and oil palm; though oil palm has been contributing to a lower rate of deforestation compared to logging in the past.[55]

The expansion of oil palm has now slowed down and reversed, with the total planted area falling from 5.8 million ha to 5.67 million ha between 2017 and 2022. Also, Malaysia's forest cover comprises 55 per cent or 18.05 million ha of total land area, which is more than the 50 per cent commitment required at the Earth Summit of 1992.[56] Oil palm plantations in Malaysia since the 1990s have been planted on land converted from other crops as farmers switch to oil palm for higher yields and profit, though its exact percentage cannot be ascertained.

Malaysia and Indonesia both have laws that limit the percentage of land that can be used for agriculture, oil palm-related land clearing and deforestation.[57] As of December 2022, 87.7 per cent of total independent

---

[53] Tang and Al Qahtani, "Sustainability of Oil Palm Plantations in Malaysia", p. 5004.

[54] Ibid., p. 5006.

[55] Ibid., p. 5006.

[56] *New Straits Times*, "Oil Palm and Deforestation: Malaysia Cannot Be Considered a 'High-Risk' Country", 23 June 2023, https://www.nst.com.my/opinion/columnists/2023/06/925431/oil-palm-and-deforestation-malaysia-cannot-be- considered-high-risk (accessed 15 November 2023).

[57] Agricultural expansion for oil palm is limited to land zoned for agriculture. The effectiveness of these laws has however often been called into question as they are either deemed insufficient, riddled with loopholes or simply not enforced due to corruption, lack of manpower for monitoring and enforcement or difficulties in accessing rural areas where plantations have sprouted.

smallholders have been certified under MSPO.[58] Together with oil palm plantations and organized smallholders, more than 97 per cent of oil palms were certified by the end of January 2023.[59] All oil palm plantations are presently MSPO-certified with some independent smallholders (about 3 per cent remaining) in the process of being certified.

The European Union has featured strongly as the top export destination for palm oil and palm-based products. The importance of the EU therefore cannot be underplayed as it is a major market for both Malaysian and Indonesian palm oil and palm-based products. Any export barriers to the EU are likely to significantly impact revenues from Malaysian oil palm. Hence the recent lobbying by both Malaysia and Indonesia for the EU to remain open to oil palm exports and the battle over certification standards and recognition. While the quantity of palm oil exports might be lower than that exported elsewhere, the export of downstream products to the EU has a much higher total value. This makes the market very important to maintain.

India and China are Malaysia's next largest export markets (see Figure 5). In the export of palm oil and palm-based products in 2022 (worth a total of RM137,890.54 million), the top ten major export destinations were the European Union (EU) (15.4 per cent), India (13.4 per cent), China (11.9 per cent), Japan (4.7 per cent), Türkiye (4.3 per cent), Philippines (3.3 per cent), Kenya (3.2 per cent), Republic

---

[58] Ghulam Kadir Ahmad Parveez, Omar Abd Rasid, Mohd Najob Ahmad, Humaira Mat Taib, Mohd Azwan Mohd Bakri, Sitti Rahma Abdul Hafid, Tuan Noor Maznee Tuan Ismail, Soh Kheang Loh, Meilina Ong Abdullah, Kalsom Zakaria and Zainab Idris, "Oil Palm Economic Performance in Malaysia and R&D Progress in 2022", *Journal of Oil Palm Research* 35, no. 2 (June 2023), p. 203.

[59] *Business Today*, "More Than 97% of Oil Palm Planted Areas Are MSPO-Certified", 28 February 2023, https://www.businesstoday.com.my/2023/02/28/more-than-97-of-oil-palm-planted-areas-are-mspo-certified/#:~:text=A%20total%20of%205.5%20million,Minister%20Datuk%20Siti%20Aminah%20Aching (accessed 15 November 2023).

Figure 5: Export of Palm Oil and Palm Based Products: Top Ten Countries (Percentage of Total Value of RM137,890.54 million), 2022

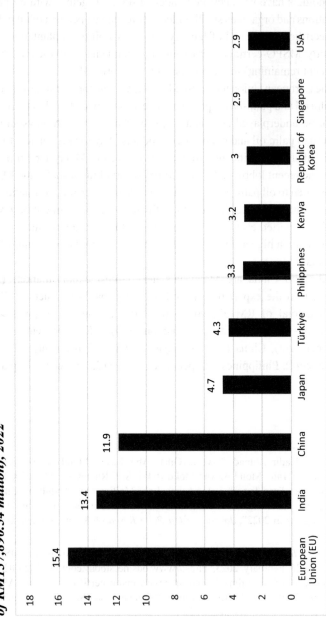

Source: Ministry of Plantation and Commodities, "Data Statistics on Commodities 2022: Palm Oil, Malaysia: 2023", p. 26, https://www.kpk.gov.my/kpk/images/mpi_statistik/2023_statistik_on_commodity/Sawit_2023.pdf (accessed 15 November 2023).

of Korea (3 per cent), Singapore (2.9 per cent) and the United States of America (2.9 per cent).[60]

In terms of just palm oil (crude palm oil) exports, India has been the top export destination followed by China and the European Union (Figure 6). For some years, the European Union was the highest export market (2018, 2019, 2020) but India and China overtook the EU in the last two years. See Appendix 2 for details from 2018 to 2022.

In June 2023, it was reported that Malaysia's Deputy Prime Minister and also then Plantations and Commodities Minister, Fadillah Yusof,[61] led a mission to meet key European Union lawmakers to seek a possible solution to its new deforestation law known as the European Union Deforestation-free Regulation (EUDR). The EUDR is expected to come into force in December 2024, which would dampen exports from Malaysia to the EU.[62] The EUDR currently does not recognize either Indonesia's or Malaysia's national sustainable certification schemes for palm oil.

One controversial requirement is the provision of traceability and geolocation paragons as it would be burdensome and challenging for smallholders to keep records for such purposes when some of these regions do not have phone lines or Internet access.[63] Clarity was also needed for its benchmarking system and land legality clauses. The

---

[60] Ministry of Plantation and Commodities, "Data Statistics on Commodities 2022: Palm Oil, Malaysia: 2023", p. 26.

[61] As of 12 December 2023, Johari Abdul Ghani has taken over as the Plantation and Commodities Minister. Fadillah Yusof remains Malaysia's Deputy Prime Minister and is now also Minister of Energy Transition and Public Utilities, following a cabinet reshuffle.

[62] *Malay Mail*, "DPM Fadillah Promotes Malaysian Palm Oil in EU, Keeping the Trade Doors Open for Smallholders", 11 June 2023, https://www.malaymail.com/news/money/2023/06/11/dpm-fadillah-promotes-malaysian-palm-oil-in-eu-keeping-the-trade-doors-open-for-smallholders/73730 (accessed 15 November 2023); and *New Straits Times*, "Ensure Palm Oil Goods Continue to Enter EU Once New Law Takes Effect Next Year", 21 November 2023, https://www.nst.com.my/business/corporate/2023/11/980747/ensure-palm-oil-goods-continue-enter-eu-once-new-law-takes-effect (accessed 2 February 2024).

[63] See *New Straits Times*, "Oil Palm and Deforestation"; and *Malay Mail*, "DPM Fadillah Promotes Malaysian Palm Oil in EU".

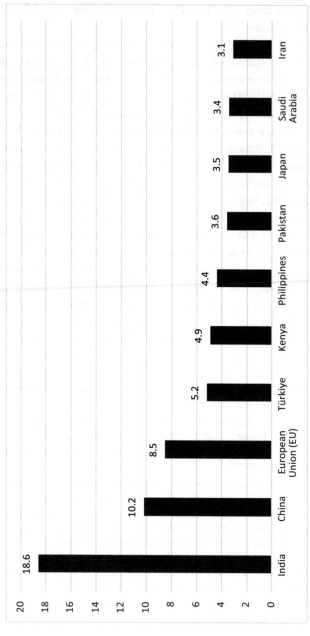

Figure 6: Export of Palm Oil: Top Ten Countries (Percentage of Total Value of RM82,493.56 million)

Source: Ministry of Plantation and Commodities, "Data Statistics on Commodities 2022: Palm Oil, Malaysia: 2023", p. 27, https://www.kpk.gov.my/kpk/images/kpk/images/2023_statistik/mpi_statistik_on_commodity/Sawit_2023.pdf (accessed 15 November 2023).

EUDR is currently viewed by Malaysia and Indonesia as another trade-discriminatory move to protect Europe's own vegetable trade oil, as palm oil has much higher yields and is cheaper compared to soy, corn and rapeseed oil produced by European producers.

As of 30 October 2023, it was reported that nearly 500,000 smallholders under the MSPO are expected to be connected to a new traceability platform. This will track and document transactions and satisfy the requirements for sustainability from source to exports in compliance with European Union legislation.[64]

TWO CERTIFICATION STANDARDS: MSPO VERSUS RSPO

Governments in Europe and North America have committed to and purchased *certified* palm oil, partly in response to public pressure and activism. Retailers such as Walmart, Marks & Spencer, Unilever, Nestle, and many others, source for only certified palm oil.[65] Climate change and global warming concerns increasingly make sustainability the main calling card for market access to many developed countries. The treatment of labour also affects saleability.[66]

---

[64] *New Straits Times*, "Sustainable Palm Oil: Nearly 500k Smallholders to Become Compliant with Platform That Traces Transactions", 30 October 2023, https://www.nst.com.my/business/economy/2023/10/972840/sustainable- palm-oil-nearly-500k-smallholders-become-compliant (accessed 24 December 2023).

[65] WWF Report, *Profitability and Sustainability in Palm Oil Production: Analysis of Incremental Financial Costs and Benefits of RSPO Compliance* (USA: WWF-USA, 2012), p. 5. https://wwfeu.awsassets.panda.org/downloads/profitability_ and_sustainability_in_palm_oil_production__update_.p df (accessed 25 July 2020).

[66] The recent account where major palm oil buyers have issued global "no buy orders" for certain Malaysian oil palm plantations because of their alleged use of forced labour shows how oil palm exports can be derailed by new kinds of threats and how important it is to address environmental and social issues in the first place. See *Straits Times*, "Buyers Shun Major Malaysian Palm Oil Producers after Forced Labour Allegations", 8 February 2021, https://www.straitstimes. com/asia/se-asia/buyers-shun-major-malaysian-palm-oil-producers-after-forced-labour- allegations (accessed 9 February 2021).

Malaysian Sustainable Palm Oil (MSPO) Certification

The MSPO standard is a national certification standard created by the Malaysian government. Beyond the Board of Trustees, a thirty-eight-member technical committee represents the various stakeholders. These stakeholders come from government, industry (upstream and downstream), smallholder organizations, environmental NGOs, civil societies, indigenous people organizations, worker unions and academia/research institutions.[67] The MSPO certification scheme is developed, managed and owned by the Malaysian Palm Oil Certification Council (MPOCC), an independent non-profit body incorporated in December 2014. A review of certification is carried out every five years to ensure relevance and effectiveness in meeting sustainability requirements. Independent smallholders, organized smallholders, plantations and all processing facilities are certified by MSPO following auditable sustainability standards accredited through third-party certification bodies.[68] While this bodes well for certification, the MPOCC is perceived as only a national certification board that inevitably wants to portray its products as sustainable.

The EU supports MSPO certification standards but sees it only as a first step towards the eventual adoption of RSPO certification, which is perceived to be all-encompassing in terms of sustainability, clear supply chain traceability, high levels of biodiversity protection, and protection of native land and worker's rights.[69] The MSPO is also deemed weaker in the protection of indigenous land rights, an issue considered very important

---

[67] K. Sanath Kumaran, Chew Jit Seng, and Balu Nambiappan, "Moving Forward with mandatory MSPO Certitification Standards", *Oil Palm Industry Economic Journal* 21, no. 10 (March 2021), p. 2. For a list of the representative members on the technical committee (38 in total), see Table 1, p. 5. The role of the technical committee is to develop, review and monitor the standards used under the MSPO certification scheme. The Board of Trustees has members from Peninsular Malaysia, Sabah and Sarawak.

[68] Ibid., p. 2.

[69] Authors' fieldwork interviews in Sabah, 31 July to 3 August 2019. See note 76.

in the European Union. However, the latest Malaysian Sustainable Palm Oil Supply Chain Certification Standard (MSPO) 2022 certification will cover the latest requirements set by the EUDR.[70] Under this revision, there is a new requirement that product players have not contributed to deforestation. Palm oil producers including smallholders will be given a grace period extending across plantations, mills and refineries to adhere to MSPO 2022 criteria by December 2024.

The Malaysian Palm Oil Board (MPOB) is responsible for organizing independent smallholders into Sustainable Palm Oil Clusters (SPOCs) and getting them ready for MSPO certification audits. MPOB also provides financial support to cover certification fees, training, chemical stores, and personnel protection equipment (PPE)[71] to smallholders working towards achieving MSPO certification. The MPOB also has the function of licensing refineries, mills and plantations; regulating the buying and selling of fresh fruit bunches; research and development; and assisting growers and industry players.[72]

In Sabah and Sarawak, the MPOB is the lead provider of support to smallholders. Producers can sell their fresh fruit bunches and receive inputs and technical support from the agency. Those not registered with MPOB in Malaysia will have to sell their produce elsewhere, usually to non-legal channels or relatives,[73] which works against the drive to achieve sustainability for the whole sector. MPOB has also assisted local

---

[70] *New Straits Times*, "Sustainable Palm Oil".

[71] This includes hand gloves, respirator, face shield and protective suits for personnel administering insecticides.

[72] Kenneth Wilson, Nicola Karen Abram, Philip Chin, Cynthia Ong, Elisna Latik, Hilary Herie Jitilon, Maslianah Ramlan, Norsuhazmil Bin Amat Nor, Chris Isham Kinsui, Mohd Dzulfikar Bin Rosli, Joannes Wasai, and Megavani Kumar, *Smallholder Readiness for Roundtable on Sustainable Palm Oil (RSPO) Jurisdictional Certification of Palm Oil by 2025: Results from Field Studies in Sabah's Telupid, Tongod, Beluran & Kinabatangan Districts* (Kota Kinabalu, Sabah: Forever Sabah, 2018), p. 66.

[73] Ibid., p. 67, and also authors' fieldwork in Sabah, 31 July to 3 August 2019, and fieldwork in Kuala Lumpur, 23 to 24 September 2019.

players in Sabah to obtain RSPO certification. In 2017, the Malaysian government announced that MSPO certification would be mandatory by 31 December 2019, a deadline subsequently extended to 2022 for smallholders. As noted above, 97 per cent of Malaysia's palm oil is now MSPO-certified. However, as these initiatives and certification schemes are to an extent industry-led, sceptics still dispute their objectivity, authenticity and effectiveness.[74]

Roundtable for Sustainable Palm Oil (RSPO) Certification

The Roundtable on Sustainable Palm Oil (RSPO) was founded by the World Wide Fund for Nature (WWF), the Malaysian Palm Oil Association (MPOA), Unilever, Migros, and AAK AB[75] in April 2004, while the RSPO certification system came into being in 2007.[76] RSPO is the only international multi-stakeholder organization to focus exclusively on sustainable palm oil. With 4,800 members worldwide as of June 2020, the RSPO represents links along the entire palm oil supply chain, including producers, civil society, processors or traders, consumer goods manufacturers, retailers, banks/investors, and governments. Many of the big-name oil palm refining, milling and plantation organizations are members of the RSPO. The organization manages myriad levels of certification in individual sectors (supply, processing, etc.) as well as in the entire supply chain, the highest form of certification available.[77]

Detractors of the RSPO and its certification system contend that, as an industry-driven initiative, it is more greenwashing than facilitating authentic sustainability. These critics cite highly publicized incidents of the organization's inability to enforce and prevent open burning by RSPO

---

[74] Nusa Urbancic, "Time Is Running out for Palm Oil Certification," *Mongabay. com*, 6 June 2018, https://news.mongabay.com/2018/06/time-is-running-out-for-palm-oil-certification-commentary/

[75] Vegetable oil solutions provider. See https://www.aak.com/about-AAK/

[76] See https://www.rspo.org/about for information on RSPO.

[77] It is possible to be an affiliate member of the RSPO for various purposes if one is not a sustainable oil palm producer. More information can be found at https://rspo.org/members/membership-categories

members or to settle land disputes with local and indigenous people as examples of its ineffectiveness.[78]

Beyond its difficulty in convincingly establishing itself as an independent entity, the RSPO also faces allegations of bias in favour of the larger industry members that purportedly drive its agenda. Obstacles placed in the way of smallholders include prohibitive technical and technological requirements (including physical infrastructure) and the high cost of certification and auditing.

Some circles claim that the RSPO has insignificant representation from environmental and social NGOs and is dominated by businesses. Although membership from oil palm producers, processors and manufacturers make up 95 per cent and outweigh NGO members, in terms of the Board of Governors, environmental and social NGOs occupy four out of the sixteen seats (25 per cent of the total), which is significant and can influence the stance of the organization.[79] Given the public scrutiny of RSPO, the organization is always on the lookout to address NGO concerns to maintain its credibility.[80]

---

[78] Refer to M.E. Cattau, M.E. Marlier, and R. DeFries, "Effectiveness of Roundtable on Sustainable Palm Oil (RSPO) for Reducing Fires on Oil Palm Concessions in Indonesia from 2012 to 2015", *Environmental Research Letters* 11, no. 10 (2016), https://iopscience.iop.org/article/10.1088/1748-9326/11/10/105007; Rainforest Action Network, "Cargill's Problems with Palm Oil: A Burning Threat in Borneo", 2018, https://www.ran.org/wp-content/uploads/2018/06/cargills_problems_with_palm_oil_low.pdf; and Retno Kusumaningtyas, "External Concern on the ISPO and RSPO Certification Schemes" (Amsterdam: Profundo, 2017), https://www.foeeurope.org/sites/default/files/eu-us_trade_deal/2018/report_profundo_rspo_ispo_external_concerns_feb2018.pdf

[79] See D. Wignand, "RSPO Certification: Implications for Smallholder Farmers", Term Paper Submitted for Environmental Management and Information Systems, Humbolt University Berlin, Winter Semester 2014/15.

[80] One of the primary mantras behind RSPO certification is its emphasis on sustainability and the protection of the environment. Principle 2 of RSPO (commitment to applicable laws and regulations), Principle 4 (use of appropriate best practices by growers and millers), and Principle 5 (environmental responsibility and conservation of natural resources and biodiversity) ensure that both community and environmental concerns will be taken into account.

To its credit, the RSPO now has a task force dedicated to smallholders, especially as global smallholder production comprises 3 million farmers worldwide.[81] There are now also a number of tools that can help smallholders overcome the financial hurdles of certification, including the RSPO Smallholder Support Fund and the jurisdictional certification scheme. There are also numerous NGOs that focus primarily on helping smallholder farmers achieve necessary certification and gain access to markets.

CERTIFICATION CHALLENGES: SABAH TAKES THE LEAD

Sabah has about 1.54 million ha of its land area cultivated with palm oil, with smallholders taking up 221,138 million ha, and estates having about 1,325,766 ha.[82] There are an estimated 53,000 smallholders in Sabah, and palm oil provides between one-third to half of their household income. Average holdings are from 3 to 7.3 ha, and smallholder median incomes are RM1,500[83] to RM2,220[84] per month, well below Sabah's median income of RM5,000 per month.[85] The RSPO defines smallholders as farmers planting on 50 ha of land and below.

---

[81] The RSPO definition of a smallholder is a landowner of less than 50 ha of land who often grows oil palm alongside subsistence or food crops. Source: https://rspo.org/smallholders

[82] Lee Poh Onn, "Saleable and Sustainable: Sabah Takes the Lead in Palm Oil Certification in Malaysia", *ISEAS Perspective*, no. 2021/106, 11 August 2021, https://www.iseas.edu.sg/wp-content/uploads/2021/07/ISEAS_Perspective_2021_106.pdf (accessed 15 November 2023). This discussion on Sabah and Sarawak draws from this perspective.

[83] Wilson et al., *Smallholder Readiness for Roundtable on Sustainable Palm Oil (RSPO) Jurisdictional Certification of Palm Oil by 2025*, p. 14.

[84] Shaufique Fahmi Sidique et al., *The Impacts of RSPO on the Livelihood of Smallholders*, pp. 39 and 59.

[85] Wilson et al., *Smallholder Readiness for Roundtable on Sustainable Palm Oil (RSPO) Jurisdictional Certification of Palm Oil by 2025*, pp. 13–14.

Sabah is the first state in Malaysia to plan for statewide RSPO certification across its plantations and smallholders, a feat that many other states have yet to follow and should perhaps emulate if they wish for wider market access. The Sabah state cabinet approved on 21 October 2015 a multi-stakeholder proposal to move Sabah to a 100 per cent RSPO-certified sustainable palm oil (CSPO) production process. This does not mean that there was no RSPO compliance before that; the difference is that those initial processes were not state-led. The Sabah Forestry Department (SFD) and the Natural Resources Office (NRO) under the Chief Minister's Department are the government co-initiators of the proposal. This was logical as the SFD has been pioneering the sustainable forest management approach since 1997.[86]

Other government agencies involved include the Environment Protection Department, the Department of Agriculture, and the Lands and Surveys Department.[87] In early 2016, the Jurisdiction Certification Steering Committee (JCSC) was established with government agencies, industry, and civil society representation, co-chaired by the SFD and NRO.[88] The RSPO and Forever Sabah acted as non-voting technical advisers at the beginning of the process. This statewide approach involving government, oil palm plantations, smallholders, NGOs, and technical advisors in the RSPO certification process is known as Jurisdictional Certified Sustainable Palm Oil (JCSPO).

The Jurisdictional Approach has four objectives: stringently protecting biodiversity in the state by achieving minimal loss of what is commonly known as High Conservation Value (HCV) forests; enabling zero conflict in oil palm producing landscapes; strengthening smallholders and

---

[86] The Sabah Forest Department is also the largest owner of oil palm plantations in the state. See Kugan, "The Implementation of the Sabah Jurisdictional Certified Sustainable Palm Oil (JCSPO) Initiative".

[87] Ibid.

[88] Industry includes Sawit Kinabalu Group, PBBOil Palms Berhad (Wilmar International), Hap Seng Plantations Holdings Berhad, and Wild Asia. The civil societies include Forever Sabah Berhad, HUTAN-KOCP, WWF Malaysia, PACOS Trust, Society of Agricultural Scientists, Sabah (SASS). Ibid.

uplifting livelihoods; as well as creating a strong institutional framework for its continuance. The goal is to bring all oil palm plantations within Sabah, including smallholders, towards RSPO certification by 2025. The funds needed to implement the JCSPO for the first five years (2016 to 2021) were RM17.8 million or US$4.2 million in 2021 dollars. Ensuring high conservation value and high carbon stock forests (HCV and HCS), to protect biodiversity around oil palm cultivated areas would cost an estimated RM4.3 million. Enabling zero conflict in forests for land rights amounts to RM3.4 million while strengthening smallholder sustainability and uplifting local livelihoods costs RM7.8 million. Establishing the proper institutional framework would amount to RM2.3 million.[89]

As the first move for Sabah to achieve state-wide and state-led RSPO certification, especially for its smallholders, four districts—Telupid, Tongod, Beluran and Kinabatangan—were selected out of twenty-three by the JCSC to explore some of the challenges involved. Forever Sabah went to the ground in these districts to identify the gaps between current indigenous practices and RSPO's environmental, social and legal standards. Table 4 highlights some of these findings.

As the mandate was for the entire country to be MSPO-certified by 2022, Sabah worked on integrating the MSPO process within the more criteria-extensive RSPO jurisdictional process. The Jurisdictional Approach in RSPO involves integrated landscape management that incorporates labour, land tenure, indigenous rights, and smallholder readiness into one holistic management plan. Sabah authorities see MSPO as providing the first step, with RSPO certification as the end goal. RSPO certification is implemented through the Jurisdictional Certification of Sustainable Palm Oil (JCSPO) process by the JCSC.

What are some of the challenges to implementing MSPO in Sabah? Land and agriculture are state matters; the decision to use land cannot be determined by the Federal government and is protected by the Malaysia

---

[89] Frederick Kugan, "Roundtable Meeting on Sustainable Palm Oil Prep. Cluster 4: Jurisdictional Approaches: Delivering Sustainable and Deforestation-Free Palm Oil", RT 16 (RSPO), Kota Kinabalu Sabah, 2018.

Table 4: Study of Smallholders in Telupid, Tongod, Beluran and Kinabatangan (TTBK)

Malaysian Palm Oil Board (Federal Agency) 1. Has been providing extensive support to smallholders, 2. Strong Presence in TTBK	• 44 per cent of smallholders in TTBK (16 of 20 villages) have been involved in some sort of MPOB programme (workshops and talks on oil palm management, including the use of fertilizer and agrochemicals). • Has helped improve the technical skills of smallholders (information sharing and implemented a palm cropping programme with cropping and livestock management). • Targeted the transfer of sustainable technology and channelled government aid schemes through TUNAS officers as extension agents (e.g. to teach "Good Agricultural Practice" or GAP). GAP is the equivalent of RSPO's "Best Management Practices".
Smallholders 1. Present status, productivity and incomes can be improved	• 81 per cent of total smallholder land is under oil palm, but yields are presently half its potential compared to elsewhere (10 t fresh fruit bunch/ha/yr). • Past 15–20 years: oil palm has become the dominant land use for smallholders over large parts of Sabah. • Average of 2.98 ha for smallholders in TTBK. Sabah has an average holding of 6.4 ha/ smallholder. • Incomes are low at about RM1,500 in TTBK, below the RM5,000 median income in Sabah.
Challenges 1. Poor access, poor agricultural support 2. Land tenure issues 3. Perception of RSPO	• Poor access to markets for Fresh Fruit Bunches. • Reliance on herbicides (not accepted by RSPO). • Fertilizers and extension services by MPOB were not increasing output, but those provided by the Sabah Department of Agriculture have doubled fresh fruit bunch yields. • Smallholders are grateful to MPOB but MPOB's effectiveness can certainly be improved. • If productivity increases by 5 per cent, Forever Sabah estimates that another RM25 million can be generated per year.

continued on next page

35

Table 4 — cont'd

4. Violation of RSPO principles—open burning, HCV, planting on peatlands, and labour issues.	• 61 per cent of smallholders in TTBK are growing oil palm on Land Application (LA) status, namely, for the land they have applied for but do not have a formal title to. Such titles are not acceptable to RSPO's FPIC process; only about 36 per cent have land titles. MPOB has registered 63 per cent (including land other than that of LA status) of the users of this untitled land for palm oil production. Smallholders without titles (but LAs) have been successfully registered with the MPOB.
	• For RSPO, the Free Prior and Informed Consent (FPIC) process is essential for land legality. FPIC is better known as *sumuka* (in the Kadazan-Dusun dialect) amongst the smallholders.
	• MPOB, although a Federal Agency, is viewed by smallholders as an official government agency, whereas RSPO is not.
	• Only 17 per cent have heard of RSPO, but two-thirds of these would like to become RSPO-certified. The main reservation is their financial situation and the costs involved in certification. Main gains in certification are to resolve land tenure issues, gain a secure Native Title on Land Application areas where they had already planted, and increase productivity. Of 137 smallholders, 87 per cent use slash and burn to clear land, while some use existing cleared areas such as old paddy fields.
	• Areas classified as High Conservation Value (HCV) cannot be cleared. 40 per cent of interviewed have cleared HCV land. HCV is a categorization of land, usually under forest cover requiring special management measures according to RSPO and the Forest Stewardship Council.
	• 17 per cent of the land used is on peat, also forbidden in RSPO; 50% of smallholders experience wildlife conflicts on their oil palm plantations.
	• 20 to 30 per cent of smallholders in TTBK hire illegal labour.

Source: Adapted from Kenneth Wilson, Nicola Karen Abram, Philip Chin, Cynthia Ong, Elisna Latik, Hilary Herie Jitilon, Maslianah Ramlan, Norsuhazmil Bin Amat Nor, Chris Isham Kinsui, Mohd Dzulfikar Bin Rosli, Joannes Wasai, and Megavani Kumar, *Smallholder Readiness for Roundtable on Sustainable Palm Oil (RSPO) Jurisdictional Certification of Palm Oil by 2025: Results from Field Studies in Sabah's Telupid, Tongod, Beluran & Kinabatangan Districts* (Kota Kinabalu, Sabah: Forever Sabah, 2018), pp. 13–27; substantiated by author's fieldwork interviews in Sabah, 31 July to 3 August 2019; see also Lee Poh Onn, "Saleable and Sustainable: Sabah Takes the Lead in Palm Oil Certification in Malaysia", *ISEAS Perspective*, no. 2021/106, 11 August 2021, pp. 7–8, https://www.iseas.edu.sg/wp-content/uploads/2021/07/ISEAS_Perspective_2021_106. pdf (accessed 15 November 2023).

Agreement 1963. Therefore, when the MSPO was made mandatory, this was initially not well received in Sabah, which saw the management of its palm oil areas as a state right.[90] However, the Department of Agriculture in Sabah is understaffed, is unable to take the lead, and lacks complete expertise to manage oil palm.[91] Agricultural support for oil palm production has therefore been mainly provided by the MPOB.

MSPO certification was also perceived as a "top-down" initiative arising from a federal body in Peninsular Malaysia; this was regarded with suspicion by segments of the Sabahan community. Smallholders have however viewed MPOB more positively as a national government initiative with a promise of funds and resources.[92]

In some quarters, it was felt that the MSPO certification process does not impose the same exacting standards as that of the RSPO—notably the latter's greater recognition of indigenous land rights (see FPIC under "Challenges" in Table 4 of this paper) and its more stringent efforts on conservation in high biodiversity areas (see HCV under "Challenges" in Table 4).[93] Under the RSPO, smallholders must have formal land titles to their oil palm areas, whereas this is not explicitly required under the MSPO (see MPOB under "Challenges" in Table 4).[94] The move to see MSPO as a necessary and crucial first step complementing RSPO enables Sabah to avoid "disobeying" federal directives, and allows it to prioritize agricultural concerns on its own terms by explicitly including RSPO in the certification process. The adoption of both certification standards is also not without justification. Interviews of 103 companies across Malaysia show that 70 per cent of them believe that both MSPO and

---

[90] Authors' fieldwork interviews in Sabah, 31 July to 3 August 2019.

[91] Ibid.

[92] Wilson et al., *Smallholder Readiness for Roundtable on Sustainable Palm Oil (RSPO) Jurisdictional Certification of Palm Oil by 2025*, p. 19; and authors' fieldwork interviews in Sabah, 31 July to 3 August 2019.

[93] Authors' fieldwork interviews in Sabah, 31 July to 3 August 2019.

[94] Authors' fieldwork interviews in Kuala Lumpur, 23 to 24 September 2019.

RSPO should be made mandatory in Malaysia.[95] To date, about 26 per cent of Sabah-produced palm oil is RSPO-certified.

Importantly, consideration must be given to the costs of implementing RSPO certification. MSPO's certification costs are less than RSPO's, as land assessments for and continual management of High Conservation Value (HCV) areas are not prerequisites.[96] Repeated Environmental Impact Assessments (EIA) in existing MSPO-certified plantations are also not required.[97] RSPO costs include identification, preparation, setting aside, and active management of HCV areas within plantations, as well as the costs of conducting both the EIA and social impact assessment (SIA). In the RSPO process, internal and external audits must be undertaken to verify and record the estate's improved production, conservation standards, and corrective actions taken in its later years of operation. Companies must also demonstrate that they have a legitimate right to use the land and that the plantation or smallholder has a legal right to plant in that area.

Costs for certifying palm oil involving HCV, EIA and SIA (including initial land assessment and subsequent certification over twenty-five years) have been estimated at about RM851 million per year for a total area of 5,392,235 ha; this amounts to about RM157.82 per ha per year for meeting RSPO requirements.[98] While there is an RSPO Independent Smallholder Fund (RISF), whose task is to help and support smallholders to improve livelihoods and practices towards achieving certification,

---

[95] Noorhayati Mansor, Wan Amalina Wan Abdullah, Asniati Bahari, and Alif Falni Hassan Syukri, "Palm Oil Sustainability Certification and Firm Performance: Is There a Conflict Between RSPO and MSPO?", Conference paper presented at "The European Business and Management Conference 2016", Brighton: United Kingdom, 2016.

[96] RSPO is a member of ISEAL but MSPO is not. For more information on ISEAL, see https://www.isealalliance.org

[97] Under MSPO, only new plantings exceeding 500 ha require an EIA.

[98] Yusof Basiron and Foong-Kheong Yew, "The Burden of RSPO Certification Costs on Malaysia Palm Oil Industry and National Economy", *Journal of Oil Palm, Environment & Health* 7 (2016), p. 23.

there is no guarantee that these often economically disadvantaged smallholders will be able to afford the costs of certification.[99] Presently, the uptake for certified oil palm is about 50 per cent. Hence, only 50 per cent of palm oil enjoys a price premium; this will need to be increased to incentivize the production of certified oil palm.

Benefits of RSPO Certification

What are the benefits of RSPO certification?[100] A study of smallholders in Sabah and Sarawak who have completed certification[101] identified these to be in the form of spillover effects to non-certified smallholders in Sapi (Sabah) and also in Keresa (Sarawak), and in the form of learning about good agricultural practices from their certified counterparts.[102] Non-RSPO farmers have gained from the close social relationship and connectedness of living in the same community with certified smallholders and the infrastructure provided by plantations nearby. Second, the mean income for certified households has been 10 per cent higher in Sapi and 25 per cent higher in Keresa, than for their non-RSPO counterparts.

In Sapi, it appears that 93 per cent of smallholders are aware of RSPO but have little idea of what it entails. Most respondents in Sapi have heard about RSPO by 2013 and 2014. In Keresa, it was in 2012 that most respondents heard about RSPO.[103] The reasons smallholders in Sabah and Sarawak apply for RSPO certification have been the incentive to sell their fresh fruit bunches at a premium price, improve farm yield, manage their farms more efficiently, learn about sustainable farming and improve

---

[99] Authors' fieldwork interviews in Kuala Lumpur, 23 to 24 September 2019.

[100] This section draws from Lee Poh Onn, "Saleable and Sustainable".

[101] A total of 76 and 100 smallholders were interviewed in Keresa and Sapi respectively.

[102] Keresa is located in the Bintulu district of Sarawak. Sapi is located in the Sandakan district. See Shaufique Fahmi Sidique et al., *The Impacts of RSPO on the Livelihood of Smallholders*, p. 2.

[103] Ibid., p. 26.

household incomes.[104] In Sabah, the Wild Asia Group Scheme (WAGS), in collaboration with the Malaysian Palm Oil Board's Smallholder Palm Oil Cluster (MPOB SPOC), organized and assisted these smallholders towards RSPO certification and good agricultural practices.[105] At the same time, Wilmar International Limited has supported this initiative through its Sapi Palm Oil Mill in the area. In this set-up, the multi-stakeholder collaboration between smallholders, an NGO (Wild Asia), the government (MPOB), and an agribusiness group (Wilmar International) was one factor that ensured the success of certification in this area, serving as an example for others to follow.

In Sarawak, Keresa Plantations and Mill became RSPO-certified in October 2010,[106] and independent smallholders near the plantation became RSPO-certified under the Keresa Smallholders Group Scheme (KSGS) in 2011. The KSGS created a positive synergy whereby Keresa Plantations and Mill helped smallholders by providing extension services to smallholders in its vicinity in the form of guidance, training and also credit facilities.[107]

By 2014, twenty-three smallholders in Sapi were already certified while forty-four were waiting to be certified; they were incidentally among the first to be certified in Sabah. Farmers in this area had already stopped open burning and were clearing their land manually through slashing and were using herbicide to prepare their land for planting. As per RSPO requirements and training from WAGS, these farmers used less herbicide to clear the land than non-certified smallholders tend to do. In Keresa, twenty-eight out of forty-two applicants achieved certification in 2012. Smallholders in Keresa are the first group of independent smallholders in Malaysia certified by RSPO.[108] Likewise, by 2012, no open burning was reported in Keresa for the opening up of new land.[109]

---

[104] Ibid., p. 62.

[105] Ibid., p. 16.

[106] Ibid., p. 15.

[107] Ibid.

[108] Ibid., p. 27.

[109] Ibid., p. 30.

There was also better handling of chemical inputs among certified smallholders, resulting in the general belief that RSPO certification was beneficial to their natural environment in Sapi. Although Sapi smallholders' incomes were higher than those of non-certified smallholders, their output was however lower when compared to that of the latter. In Sapi, the average household income for all respondents was RM26,737 per year. RSPO-certified farmers had the highest income of RM28,834, followed by those waiting to be certified (RM28,072), and non-certified members (RM26,123). Most smallholders were also close to the mill, hence their harvests could be delivered cost-effectively there.[110] In Keresa, certified farmers also applied less herbicide, contributed by practical information learned from the training programmes provided by KSGS. In Keresa, certified RSPO members earned RM23,922 per annum compared to non-RSPO members who earned RM20,848 per annum.[111]

Underinvestment in fertilizers was identified as one possible cause and this arose from the inadequate extension services provided by WAGS in Sabah.[112] Continuous education and support need to be provided to improve the impact of RSPO certification on smallholders' livelihoods. Certified mills could provide these extension services in exchange for a continuous supply of fresh fruit bunches. Premium pricing of fresh fruit bunches has attracted more smallholders to join RSPO. Certified mills (like Wilmar International and Sime Darby) are transparent in their grading, pricing and payment for fresh fruit bunches and can continue to help in the certification process. In Sabah, some millers have yet to support smallholders in the certification process and a significant percentage of smallholders are in conflict areas (with no formal land titles).[113] As such, RSPO cannot proceed with certifying in such land areas.

---

[110] Ibid., p. 59.

[111] Ibid., p. 39.

[112] Ibid., p. 58.

[113] Authors' fieldwork interviews in Kuala Lumpur, 23 to 24 September 2019.

CONCLUSION

The economic significance of palm oil in Malaysia cannot be disputed. As such, the proposed ban by the EU on unsustainable sources is a concern to Indonesia and Malaysia, both of which have their own national certification systems, which are not recognized internationally. The implementation of the international RSPO system is promising. It has wider acceptance, including in the EU, but it also poses challenges in terms of costs.

This paper has shown how Sabah is actively taking the lead to ensure that its oil palm plantations (of all sizes) are sustainably certified. Cooperation and collaboration between multiple stakeholders of all levels have shown some positive success. Sabah also has examples, of Yet Hing Plantations and the Melangking Oil Palm Plantation Company, which are actively embracing sustainability principles without joining RSPO, as well as experimenting to improve their positive contributions to surrounding local communities and natural areas, and working with scientists to experiment with multi-cropping, regardless of their certification status.[114] This in itself may warrant a separate case study in the future.

These grassroots and state government-led efforts bode well for the future of sustainable oil palm in Sabah, especially since it is the world's third-largest palm oil producer. These efforts are a good model for other states to adopt in their joint efforts to improve overall sustainability and to gain global recognition for Malaysian oil palm and palm-based exports.

---

[114] Authors' fieldwork interviews in Sabah (personal communication with informant), and additional information and evidence as provided by the article: Emily Ding, "Can Plantations Value More Than Profit? Some in Malaysia Think So", *Al Jazeera*, 23 June 2023, https://www.aljazeera.com/features/2023/6/28/can-plantations-value-more-than-profit-some-in-malaysia-think-so, as well as conversations with the related scientist in the French Embassy sponsored programme, "Trails", at the Melangking Oil Palm Plantation Company during the Malaysia-France Convention in November 2023.

Appendix 1: Malaysia: Oil Palm Planted Area, 1975–2022 (hectares)

Year	Peninsular Malaysia	Sabah	Sarawak	Total
1975	568,561	59,139	14,091	641,791
1976	629,558	69,708	15,334	714,600
1977	691,706	73,303	16,805	781,814
1978	755,525	78,212	19,242	852,979
1979	830,536	86,683	21,644	938,863
1980	906,590	93,967	22,749	1,023,306
1981	983,141	100,611	24,104	1,107,863
1982	1,048,015	110,717	24,065	1,182,797
1983	1,099,694	128,248	25,098	1,253,040
1984	1,143,522	160,507	26,237	1,330,266
1985	1,292,399	161,500	28,500	1,482,399
1986	1,410,923	162,645	25,743	1,599,311
1987	1,460,502	182,612	29,761	1,672,875
1988	1,556,540	213,124	36,259	1,805,923
1989	1,644,309	252,954	49,296	1,946,559
1990	1,698,498	276,171	54,795	2,029,464
1991	1,744,615	289,054	60,359	2,094,028
1992	1,775,633	344,885	77,142	2,197,660
1993	1,831,776	387,122	87,027	2,305,925
1994	1,857,626	452,485	101,888	2,411,999
1995	1,903,171	518,133	118,783	2,540,087
1996	1,926,378	626,008	139,900	2,692,286
1997	1,959,377	758,587	175,125	2,893,089
1998	1,987,190	842,496	248,430	3,078,116
1999	2,051,595	941,322	320,476	3,313,393

continued on next page

Appendix 1 -- cont'd

Year	Peninsular Malaysia	Sabah	Sarawak	Total
2000	2,045,500	1,000,777	330,387	3,376,664
2001	2,096,856	1,027,328	374,828	3,499,012
2002	2,187,010	1,068,973	414,260	3,760,243
2003	2,202,166	1,135,100	464,774	3,802,040
2004	2,201,606	1,165,412	508,309	3,875,327
2005	2,298,608	1,209,368	543,398	4,051,374
2006	2,334,247	1,239,497	591,471	4,165,215
2007	2,362,057	1,278,244	664,612	4,304,913
2008	2,410,019	1,333,566	744,372	4,487,957
2009	2,489,814	1,361,598	839,748	4,691,160
2010	2,524,672	1,409,676	919,418	4,853,766
2011	2,546,760	1,431,762	1,021,587	5,000,109
2012	2,558,103	1,442,588	1,076,238	5,076,929
2013	2,593,733	1,475,108	1,160,898	5,229,739
2014	2,617,334	1,511,510	1,263,391	5,392,235
2015	2,659,361	1,544,223	1,439,359	5,642,943
2016	2,679,502	1,551,714	1,506,769	5,737,985
2017	2,708,413	1,546,904	1,555,828	5,811,145
2018	2,727,608	1,549,245	1,572,477	5,849,330
2019	2,769,003	1,544,481	1,586,673	5,900,157
2020	2,737,723	1,543,054	1,584,520	5,865,297
2021	2,607,847	1,523,624	1,606,261	5,737,731
2022	2,544,307	1,508,060	1,622,374	5,674,742

Source: Malaysian Oil Palm Statistics 2022, 42nd ed. (Selangor, Malaysia: Malaysian Palm Oil Board (MPOB), 2023), p. 3.

Appendix 2: Production of Crude Palm Oil by State, 2018–22 (tonnes)

	2018	2019	2020	2021	2022
Johor	3,113,455	3,142,218	3,157,647	2,851,495	2,969,525
Kedah	265,770	239,073	218,106	236,668	237,382
Kelantan	294,884	332,438	338,021	314,406	336,061
Negeri Sembilan	679,451	698,440	651,310	631,112	675,767
Pahang	2,754,382	3,019,773	2,998,600	2,795,769	3,013,127
Perak	1,861,067	1,854,050	1,840,646	1,902,382	1,866,423
Selangor	519,504	521,837	509,535	522,372	498,904
Terengganu	486,416	556,230	541,371	429,665	407,500
Other States	222,517	219,729	183,663	163,128	156,661
Sabah	5,139,356	5,037,168	4,647,375	4,361,537	4,286,665
Sarawak	4,179,339	4,237,411	4,054,339	3,907,820	4,005,425
Total	19,516,141	19,858,367	19,140,613	18,116,354	18,453,440

Source: Ministry of Plantation and Commodities, "Data Statistics on Commodities 2022: Palm Oil, Malaysia: 2023", p. 5, https://www.kpk.gov.my/kpk/images/mpi_statistik/2023_statistik_on_commodity/Sawit_2023.pdf (accessed 15 November 2023).